BLACKFOOT

Anna Rebus

Weigl

Published by Weigl Educational Publishers Limited
6325 10th Street S.E.
Calgary, Alberta, Canada   T2H 2Z9

Website: www.weigl.com
Copyright ©2011 Weigl Educational Publishers Limited

Library and Archives Canada Cataloguing in Publication
Rebus, Anna
          Blackfoot / author: Anna Rebus ; editor: Heather Kissock.
(Aboriginal peoples of Canada)
Includes index.
Also available in electronic format.
ISBN 978-1-55388-648-8 (bound).--ISBN 978-1-55388-654-9 (pbk.)
          1. Siksika Indians--Juvenile literature. I. Kissock, Heather
II. Title. III. Series: Aboriginal peoples of Canada (Calgary, Alta.)
E99.S54R422 2010   j971.004'97352   C2009-907309-9

Printed in the United States of America in North Mankato, Minnesota
1 2 3 4 5 6 7 8 9 14 13 12 11 10

062010
WEP230610

Photograph and Text Credits
Cover: Royal Ontario Museum ©ROM; Alamy: pages 7, 15; All Canada Photos: page 20; Canadian Museum of Civilization: page 12B (V-B-229, D2004-25827); Corbis:
pages 4, 8, 16, 21; Getty Images: pages 5, 10, 11, 12T, 14, 22, 23; McCord Museum: page 17; Nativestock: page 13; Rolf Hicker Photography: page 6; Royal Ontario
Museum ©ROM: pages 9T, 9M, 9B.

We gratefully acknowledge the financial support of the Government of Canada through the Canada Book Fund for our publishing activities.

PROJECT COORDINATOR Heather Kissock

DESIGN Terry Paulhus

ILLUSTRATOR Martha Jablonski-Jones

Contents

4   **The People**

6   **Blackfoot Homes**

8   **Blackfoot Clothing**

10   **Hunting and Gathering**

12   **Blackfoot Tools**

14   **Moving from Place to Place**

16   **Blackfoot Music and Dance**

18   **The Old Man and the Beaver**

20   **Blackfoot Art**

22   **Activity**

24   **Glossary**

24   **Index**

The People

The Blackfoot are an **indigenous nation** that lives in Alberta, Canada, and Montana, United States. The nation is made up of three main groups, the Siksika, the Kainai, and the Piikani. Together, these groups are called the Blackfoot **Confederacy**.

Today, many Blackfoot live in towns and cities in southern Alberta. Some Blackfoot also live on reserves, or land set aside by the government for **First Nations**.

NET LINK
To find out what the Blackfoot call themselves, go to **www.glenbow.org/blackfoot**.

Blackfoot Homes

TEEPEES

In the past, the Blackfoot relied on teepees for shelter. Teepees are cone-shaped buildings made out of long tree poles. They are covered by animal hides that have been sewn together.

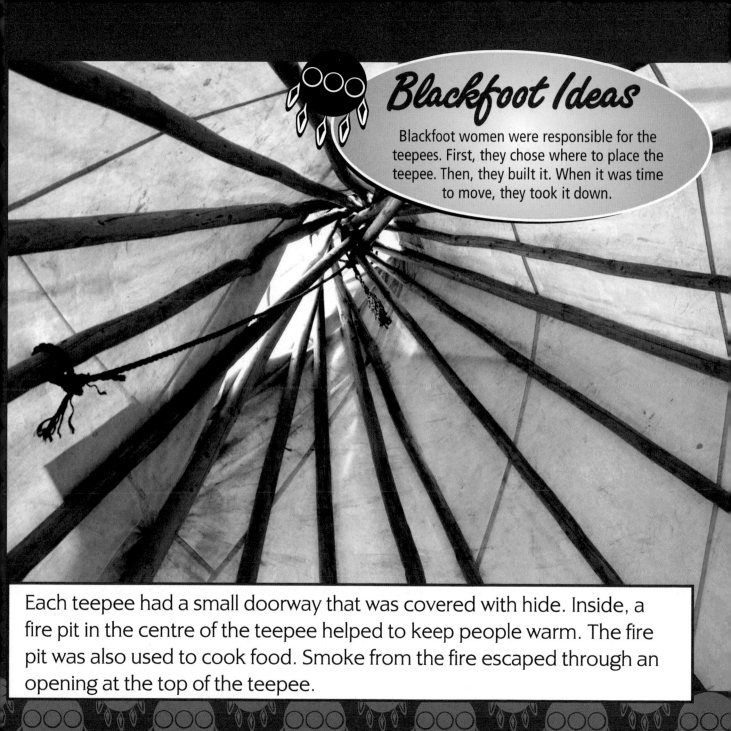

Blackfoot Ideas

Blackfoot women were responsible for the teepees. First, they chose where to place the teepee. Then, they built it. When it was time to move, they took it down.

Each teepee had a small doorway that was covered with hide. Inside, a fire pit in the centre of the teepee helped to keep people warm. The fire pit was also used to cook food. Smoke from the fire escaped through an opening at the top of the teepee.

Blackfoot Clothing

DECORATION

The Blackfoot used items found in nature to decorate their clothing. This included feathers and porcupine quills. When Europeans arrived, the Blackfoot also used glass beads.

SHIRTS AND LEGGINGS

Blackfoot men wore leggings and a shirt. These clothes were often made from elk or bison hide.

HEADDRESSES

The Blackfoot wore headdresses that were made of feathers that stood straight up.

DRESSES

Women wore one-piece dresses, with short leggings underneath. These clothes were made from animal hides.

MOCCASINS

Both men and women wore moccasins on their feet. Like their other clothing, these shoes were made from animal hide.

Hunting and Gathering

BISON

Bison meat could be boiled, roasted, or dried and mixed with berries to make **pemmican**. The pemmican was stored for use over the winter.

ONIONS

Wild onions could be eaten raw or put in stews with meat and other vegetables. The onion bulbs could also be used to make tea.

The Blackfoot depended on the bison as their main food source. They followed the bison from place to place, so they did not grow crops like many other First Nations. Instead, they ate the many different plants that grew in nature.

BERRIES

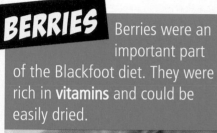

Berries were an important part of the Blackfoot diet. They were rich in **vitamins** and could be easily dried.

CAMAS

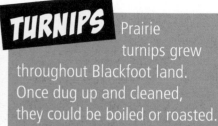

Camas bulbs were roasted in fire pits. When cooked, a camas bulb tastes like a sweet potato. It also has a sweet syrup.

TURNIPS

Prairie turnips grew throughout Blackfoot land. Once dug up and cleaned, they could be boiled or roasted.

Blackfoot Tools

ARROWHEADS

Blackfoot men made arrowheads from stone. The men carefully chipped away at the stone to make the arrowheads. They sharpened the edges of the arrowheads by removing small flakes of stone with deer or elk antlers.

Blackfoot Ideas

Other tools the Blackfoot used included knives and axes. These were made from stone, wood, and bone.

SHIELDS

Blackfoot men made shields out of bison hide. The shields were so strong they could stop an arrow.

Moving from Place to Place

TRAVOIS

When moving from one place to another, the Blackfoot carried their belongings on a travois. This was a sled made up of two poles that were joined together by a platform.

At first, dogs were used to pull the travois. Later, Europeans brought horses to the area. The Blackfoot began using these animals to pull their travois.

NET LINK

Find out how horses changed the size of the travois by surfing to **www.thecanadianencyclopedia.com**. Type "travois" into the search engine.

Blackfoot Music and Dance

Powwows were an important part of Blackfoot **culture**. At a powwow, the Blackfoot gathered to share their music, stories, and dances. Both men and women performed dances. Dancers often wore bright and colourful costumes.

Blackfoot Ideas

Today, the Blackfoot often invite other First Nations to come to their powwows.

Dancing was done to the beat of a drum. Men sat in a circle around the drum and pounded it with drumsticks. The men sang songs as they beat the drum.

NET LINK

Read about different Blackfoot dances at **www.blackfootcrossing.ca/dance.html**.

The Old Man and the Beaver

There once was an old man who loved to eat beaver meat. He hunted beavers every day. His son warned him that the beavers would become angry with him and could hurt him. The old man paid no attention and continued his hunting.

One day, the old man saw a beaver slip into a hole along the riverbank. He dove into the river to find it. The old man's son saw his father dive into the river and followed him into the hole. He grabbed his father by the feet and pushed him farther into the hole.

The old man became frightened. He thought that he was being attacked by another beaver. He begged the beaver to let him go and gave the beaver his knife and other hunting tools in exchange for his freedom. Finally, the old man was released, and he returned home.

When he entered his teepee, his son asked him where his hunting tools were. The old man told his son that he had given them to the beaver in exchange for his life. His son nodded, saying, "I told you they would catch you." The old man never hunted beaver again.

Blackfoot Art

The Blackfoot used art to record their history. Sometimes, they painted or carved images onto rocks. These images often showed an important event, such as a great battle or a successful hunt.

Blackfoot Ideas

The Blackfoot mixed clay, water, and fat to make paint. Seeds, leaves, and roots could be added to colour the paint.

The Blackfoot also painted their history onto animal hides. These hides were called winter counts.

Make Pemmican

Materials
   1 cup jerky, either beef or deer
   1 cup dried blueberries
   1 cup un-roasted sunflower seeds or crushed
      nuts of any kind
   2 teaspoons honey
   1/4 cup peanut butter

Directions
1. Grind or pound the jerky to a powder.
2. Add the dried berries and seeds or nuts.
3. Heat the honey and peanut butter until softened. Blend.
4. When cooled, store in a plastic bag in a cool, dry place.
5. Eat as a snack.

Glossary

confederacy: a union of people

culture: the arts, beliefs, and habits of a community, people, or country

First Nations: members of Canada's Aboriginal community who are not Inuit or Métis

indigenous nation: a group of people who are the original inhabitants of an area

pemmican: a mixture of dried meat and berries that has been pounded into powder and mixed with fat

vitamins: substances that help the body grow and remain healthy

art 20, 21

clothing 8, 9

dancing 16, 17

food 7, 10, 11

music 16, 17

teepee 6, 7

tools 12, 13

travois 14, 15